Great Interpreters Don't Grow On Trees:

123 Steps to the Top of the Sign Language Interpreting Field

Kelley C. Clark, MSW

D1159150

Edited by Jennifer Bondurant.

Cover design by Jennifer Johnson.

Printed by The Ovid Bell Press
Fulton, Missouri

ISBN 0-9762407-0-X

acknowledgements

I must express my gratitude to several great people for their contributions, expertise, and support, without which this book would still be cycling through my head.

Jo Ellen Clark, my sister, spent hours reviewing my work, offered suggestions and new ideas, field-tested the strategies with Rochester, New York interpreters, and provided unrelenting encouragement for my continued work.

Sandy Drummond oversaw the first and final drafts. With her eagle-sharp eyes, Sandy was exceptionally adept at both calling attention to, and finding solutions for, areas requiring changes and updates.

Many central Missouri interpreters graciously allowed me to elicit ideas by observing and, later, discussing their work.

Marla Broetz and Lori DeWindt, both Deaf, reviewed many sections of this book and provided guidance regarding cultural perspectives. They brought to light several areas I had not considered, thus bringing better balance to the book as a whole.

I am ceaselessly grateful to have my life partner, Carolyn Ball, without whom I would not be where I am today.

All of the above mentioned people were eager to help with the development of this book. However, any mistakes are all mine.

And, finally, I must thank my four Deaf great-grandparents for setting the stage, upon which I am about to stand.

contents

introduction

This book was written for practicing interpreters who intend to improve their work product. Interpreters are extraordinary, and to be successful, sign language interpreters must have a skill base as varied as the world is diverse. We are constantly faced with multi-faceted challenges and strive to produce equivalent meanings between languages and cultures while taking into account any number of a person's sociodemographic descriptors. We are charged with an incredible task and should be commended for our perseverance and sheer determination to get up and go to work everyday.

To improve our work, we diligently strive to enhance skills and techniques we have thus far acquired. In addition, we must seek out proficiencies we have yet to acquire and incorporate them into our interpretation. My hope is that this book will become a hub, a center from which many creative learning paths begin.

instructions & housekeeping

Many tasks are outlined in this book, and each one requires action above and beyond simply reading this book. Readers will be instructed to locate materials, find mentors, team interpret, and prepare before assignments. And, as if that was not enough, you will make the most of your critical thinking skills before, during, and after assignments.

To use this book, select one of the 123 strategies, read it thoroughly, and incorporate the outlined instructions into your daily routine. Work on no more than one skill per day. Choose a skill that you both want to work on and that suits your particular brand of interpreting on that day. Then, put the book down and work on only those details outlined in the section.

You may work on any skill for one day, one week, or one month. Feel free to delve deeper into any idea. Seek out related works by the many accomplished researchers and instructors in our field. I included a bibliography and list of selected materials at the end of the book for your use.

Take inspiration from even your smallest increments of skill advancement. Do not become discouraged if you do not find success on the first, second, third, or even the fourth try. Many of these skills will take years to master, and your first step to mastery begins here….

a note about vocabulary

In the book, the word "deaf" represents deaf people, Deaf people, hard of hearing people, and late-deafened adults. The word "Deaf" represents only members of the Deaf Community and/or those who identify themselves as culturally Deaf.

transcription conventions

Symbol	Explanation
#LETTERS	Fingerspelled loan sign/Lexicalized spelling – A combination of signs for English letters and ASL movements. Examples: #EARLY, #BACK, #JOB, or #BUS
F-I-N-G-E-R-S-P-E-L-L-I-N-G	Full fingerspelling. Examples: L-O-R-I S-M-I-T-H (Person's name) W-A-R A-N-D P-E-A-C-E (Book title)
+	Repetition of a sign. Example: THINK++
SMALL CAPITAL LETTERS	English glosses of signs. Example: INTERPRETER
HYPHENATED-WORDS	Two signs making a compound sign. Examples: THREE-WEEKS or FOUR-DAYS

Proactive Skill-Building While On the Job

Peter Drucker said, "There is an enormous number of managers who have retired on the job." Don't retire on the job. Skills and techniques outlined in Chapter One are to be practiced while in the act of interpreting.

1. Identify the Speakers
2. Me Kudos
3. Communication Control
4. Lag Time
5. Mind Mapping
6. Handouts
7. Completing Signs
8. Assigned Locations
9. A Ban on Speed Spelling
10. Speaking Clearly
11. Timeline Accuracy
12. Fingerspelling Location
13. No Bluffing
14. Generational Language Choices
15. Number Clarity
16. Lexicalized Fingerspelling/Loan Signs
17. Signed Transitions
18. Spoken Transitions
19. Message Comprehension
20. A Ban on Bouncing Fingerspelling
21. Consecutive Interpreting
22. Early Birding
23. But I Don't Make Mistakes!

1. Identify the Speakers

In a small, medium or large group, identify all speakers or signers as they begin their comments. Armed with knowledge of who is speaking, a deaf person is better connected to the people and events and will be in a better position to evaluate and categorize participant comments.

To identify speakers successfully, you may need to rely on name plates placed in front of the person. Prior to the meeting, ask someone for the names of all parties involved, or pay attention during introductions. Identify them by clothing, facial characteristics, or name signs. Do not be afraid to point. If pointing is ineffective, find a method that works. If you have a team interpreter, ask him or her to draw a seating chart during introductions and ask that he or she place the chart directly in front of you to establish a convenient visual aid.

2. Me Kudos

Evaluate your interpreting work immediately after each assignment. Make a written list of all the things you did right. What was effectively interpreted and why did it work? Prepare to feel good about it. Avoid dismissing accurate interpretations as flukes or attributing them to luck. Neumann-Solow (2004) said, "There is no rule that says we can't feel good about ourselves." Journal your successes in the back of your appointment book and refer to them when having an off day or when considering skills to demonstrate when mentoring others.

Finally, and this step is just as important as the previous steps, go out and reward yourself for a job well done.

3. Communication Control

Assert yourself when needed in order to facilitate communication. The interpreting process takes time, and due to the nature of interpreting, it is common for neither party to know exactly where you are in the message delivery. Tell the speaker or signer if you have not had enough time to interpret everything said or signed. Identify the uninterpreted portion or where you left off, and let him/her start there again if he or she so chooses.

Another way to control the flow of information is to softly say one or two words you are signing, letting the hearing party know what part of his or her message is being signed at that particular time. The same can be true when interpreting a signer's message. By subtly signing one or two concepts, the signer is alerted to what part of his or her message is currently being interpreted, and this cue allows the person an opportunity to slow down or reiterate subsequently signed information.

Be aware, though, that if you choose to softly say or subtly sign a few concepts, you will interrupt his or her train of thought. If you have a team interpreter, they too can be responsible for telling consumers you need extra time.

4. Lag Time

Wait until you understand an entire concept, or chunk of information, before beginning your interpretation. Your use of lag time is critical to the accuracy of the interpreted message. Cokley (1992) found, "The greater the lag time, the more information available; the more information available, the greater the level of comprehension."

Suppressing and controlling the urge to *do something* can take the strength of ten Clydesdales. Resist the pressure you feel from the anticipating participants. Trust in your memory retention skills. Once you have a handle on your use of lag time, you may notice less time spent repairing incorrectly interpreted information and an improvement in the accuracy and cohesion of the interpreted message.

5. Mind Mapping

Today, make a mind map for one upcoming job in your book. Mind mapping, also called concept mapping, is a useful tool for making information readily accessible to you and easier to retrieve. Calder (2002) explains that to make a mind map, a person writes down a central idea or concept and considers ideas that radiate out from the center. Focus on key ideas and then look for connections between the ideas. Calder goes on to explain that you are mapping knowledge in a manner that will help you understand and remember new information. Your mind map will be used as a prediction tool. Who will be involved in your upcoming job and what might their respective goal(s) be? What topics are likely to be discussed? What vocabulary is likely to be used?

For example, on the first day of interpreting an undergraduate World Civilization class, you would begin your map by placing "World Civilization" in the center. As the class proceeds, spokes projecting out from the center will include ideas specific to studying civilizations. Concepts might include: continents and countries, peoples, languages, timelines including Before the Common Era (BCE) and Common Era (CE), governments, religions, and more.

Finally, prominent researchers in our field have linked mind mapping to training interpreters. I encourage you to seek out research by Elizabeth Winston and Christine Monikowski (2000).

An Example of a Mind Map for a World Civ Class

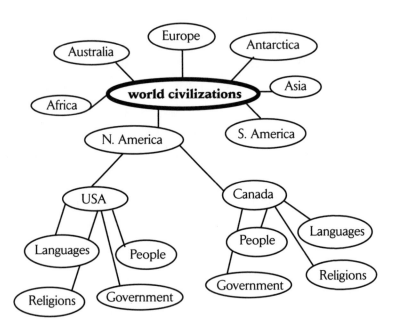

6. Handouts

When interpreting for a lecture or other speech, get any handouts available. Ask for copies of everything the audience gets either in advance or, at the very least, when everyone else gets them. Armed with handouts, you can follow along with the lecture and use them as a visual aid to reference a position on a diagram. By pointing to the referenced materials, you can save processing time and interpreting time – time that can be better used to convey more information.

You should also request handouts for your team interpreter. If he or she is interpreting, prepare the handouts for his or her use by flipping to the right page or pointing to an appropriate diagram.

7. Completing Signs

Pay attention to the clarity and complete production of your signs. Sign clarity improves ease of understanding. The parameters of a sign are its handshape, palm orientation, movement, location, and non-manual markers (Lucas, Bayley, and Valli, 2003). Today, pay close attention to the accuracy of the shapes of your hands, the directions of your palms, the actions or motions of your hands, your hand positioning, and your facial expressions. Pretend that sloppy signing is illegal today, punishable by death by firing squad.

Complete all your signs and include no extraneous movements. Observe and determine if your signs are choppy. Do you start a sign, then stop in the middle of its completion, and prematurely move on to the next sign? If so, focus on completing each sign before starting subsequent signs. Ask a team interpreter or language mentor for monitoring assistance.

8. Assigned Locations

Pay attention to where you place things in your sign space, and do not refer to them in any other location – unless you have clearly expressed the change in placement. Once locations of people, places, or things are assigned in the space surrounding an interpreter, they should be held constant until the interpreter moves or otherwise changes them (Taylor, 1993).

This placement includes the lists you make on your fingertips. Don't put Suzy on your thumb and then later refer to her in Joe's place already located on your pinky finger. Moreover, if working with a team interpreter, make sure that you put people, places and things in the same locations that your team interpreter put them.

9. A Ban on Speed-Spelling

Today, there will be no speed spelling. It is more important to be understood than to be fast. If your fingers are too fast to read, you waste precious interpreting time and you make the deaf person waste energy trying to understand something that is impossible to read. On the opposite end, avoid spelling too slowly because you might distract or annoy the addressee, or you might appear patronizing (Taylor, 1993).

10. Speaking Clearly

Clearly articulate each word. If the signer is smooth and steady, your spoken interpretation should be smooth and steady. Ensure your voice is both loud enough and projected toward the hearing consumers relying on your interpretation. Focus on the use of proper voice inflection. If you are uncertain about the message content, your vocal pitch may rise and make a signer's definitive statement sound like a question, or you may rush through a chunk of information just to get it over with. Give yourself permission to slow the communication process and/or ask for clarification. Speak more slowly. Inform the signer if you need extra time to complete the message accurately.

11. Timeline Accuracy

Today, pay attention to the accuracy of your signed timelines. If interpreted incorrectly, an event that occurred last week can look like an event that happened months or years ago, and an event scheduled to occur next week can appear as if it will happen further into the future.

For timelines, think of your body as point zero, the present tense. When discussing events on a timeline, follow Baker-Shenk and Cokley's instruction (1991). They explain you can indicate events occurring in the future by moving your hands in a forward direction. The farther your hands are from your body, the farther into the future you are illustrating. The opposite is true for events occurring in the past. Your hands will sign farther away from your body in a backward direction proportionate to when the event occurred.

In addition to the signs produced, make sure your non-manual markers are accurate.

12. Fingerspelling Location

When fingerspelling today, pay attention to where you place your hand. Battison (2003) showed the standard place for fingerspelling below the signer's chin and in front of the dominant shoulder. Keep your spelling zone consistent by beginning at that same position each time you spell. If you are right-handed, spell out and to the right. Spelling toward the middle of your body is inaccurate. Keep your elbow in and close to your body.

C. Ball (personal communication, August 15, 2004), president of the Conference of Interpreter Trainers (2000-2004), says you can practice keeping your elbow close to your body by placing a piece of paper between your arm and your torso. Hold the paper and fingerspell without dropping the paper.

13. No Bluffing

Today, no guessing or bluffing while secretly praying your interpretation is correct and pans out as you predicted. While signing or voicing, there may be times when you have no idea what one party has just said or signed. Take a deep breath and give yourself the latitude to request more information. Practice language negotiation, informing the speaker or signer that you do not understand the message or missed a point, and tell them exactly which part you missed.

For example, imagine you are interpreting a friendly conversation between Mr. LeCompte (deaf) and Ms. Dustin (non-deaf). As the conversation goes along, you might miss the state Mr. LeCompte visited. Rather than choosing to guess or omit the information altogether you ask him to repeat the name of the state. Your only goal today is to avoid all guesswork. Ask for clarification as many times as necessary to get the message right.

Several deaf people have told me they would prefer interpreters get the message right, no matter how many times we ask for clarification, in lieu of watching our body language awkwardly shift, indicating we might have missed something but are continuing anyway.

14. Generational Language Choices

Language use varies according to age. Today, tailor your interpreted word and sign choices to the generation with which you are working. An 80-year-old hearing person is not likely to use the most current slang, partly because slang goes in and out of popularity so quickly. Therefore, you need to consider different word choices when interpreting to and for him or her.

When matching age categories to English language choices, you should also consider signs that have changed over the years and be prepared to use them when the need arises. For example, an 80-year-old deaf person may choose older signs for MOVIE and TELEPHONE. Allocate time to discuss age-appropriate sign and word choices with a peer and/or a language mentor.

15. Number Clarity

Pay special attention to numbers today, including phone numbers, account numbers, math numbers, and more. Produce them so the recipient clearly sees the difference between 8 and 18 or 74 and 84. If you do nothing else right today, make sure the numbers you interpret are clearly and accurately produced.

16. Lexicalized Fingerspelling/Loan Signs

Loan signs permeate ASL. Today, look at your language use and increase your awareness of your loan sign usage. Loan signs include the following: #YES, #NO, #JOB, #BANK, #DO, #COOL, #BUS, #FIX, #CLUB, #EARLY and #HURT. By increasing your awareness of loan signs, you improve your chances of memory retrieval when you must voice or sign them. Technically, you are not fingerspelling because they are ASL signs made from borrowed vocabulary (Taylor, 2002).

If you have a team interpreter, identify and count how many times he or she uses loan signs and ask him or her to do the same for you. Seek out and watch videos on loan signs with a peer and/or a language mentor.

17. Signed Transitions

When interpreting the spoken word to a deaf person, distinct, observable transitions between themes will improve the clarity of your interpretation. In ASL, one way to separate topics is to make lists on your fingers. Begin the list with your thumb and with each subsequent point move onto the next finger, working toward your pinky finger. Interpret the information in your thumb "section," end it, and then show a change in topic by moving on to your index finger.

Other ways to show a topic change is to shift your head, body, or eye gaze. Think of other ways to show the new point, and incorporate as many as you can into your work today.

18. Spoken Transitions

When interpreting a signer's message to a hearing audience, distinctly articulated transitions between topics will improve the clarity of your interpretation. In English, effective transitions include such phrases as the following: "And, on another topic…" and "I'd like to shift gears to discuss…."

Think of other ways to show you are moving to a new point, and incorporate as many as you can into your work today.

19. Message Comprehension

Interpreting is impossible if you do not understand the material being interpreted. To improve your own comprehension during the job, you may wish to do one (or several) of the following: follow along in the book, look at the papers distributed by the teachers or lecturers, and use your lag time wisely. While your team member is interpreting, practice the math being taught so you have a better understanding of the thought processes involved. List discussion concepts, or draw a mind map and share it with your team interpreter.

Your goal is to remain cognitively engaged (instead of looking at your planner, checking e-mails on your latest electronic gizmo, or leaving to take a coffee break), so you do not miss key concepts.

20. A Ban on Bouncing Fingerspelling

No bouncing fingerspelling today. Spell horizontally, allowing your wrist to move only slightly (if at all) with each additional letter. If you find your hands bouncing, use your non-dominant hand or index finger for balance.

If working with a team interpreter, ask him or her to monitor your spelling and alert you to necessary changes.

21. Consecutive Interpreting

At your appointments today, try consecutive interpreting. Take in a chunk of information from one person, stop the flow of information, and relay the information to the second person. Then, take in the second person's information, stop the flow, and relay the information to the first person. What will you notice? Yes, it will take longer. But what else? Are your interpreted messages more accurate? Are the messages more complete? Do you find it easier to articulate the message without the distraction of more information coming in at the same time? So today, do everything in your power to interpret consecutively. You might be surprised at the results.

22. Early Birding

Today, leave ten minutes earlier than you normally would for each job. If you constantly drive with your pedal to the metal, wild-eyed and white-knuckled, only to run up the stairs arriving on time but winded, your interpretation is likely to suffer while you recuperate. In addition, if you get there early you can introduce yourself to the speaker, look over the meeting agenda, and take a minute to build your nest (arrange your interpreting location to best suit your needs). When you arrive ten minutes before you normally would, your more relaxed body should positively influence your interpretation. Later, evaluate the results.

23. But I Don't Make Mistakes!

How adept are you at explaining you have made a mistake in your interpretation? Making mistakes means we are human, not interpreters in need of another vocation. What do you say and sign when you realize you have made an error? Imagine you have interpreted for fifteen minutes about HER when the presenter meant HIM? What if you misunderstood the doctor's instructions for a prescription and you need to halt the process and reinterpret the correct dose increments? Exactly what do you sign? Use key phrases such as, "What was that amount?" and "Excuse me. What day of the week was that again?"

Don't go on and on saying, "Excuse me" and "I'm sorry." As C. R. Hamilton (personal communication, January 30, 2004), a working interpreteter at age eighty-one, aptly stated, "Fix it and move along!"

Today, either in your head or on the job, practice the art of identifying your mistakes.

chapter two

Outside the Job
Skill-Building Activities

*Tasks outlined in Chapter 2 are to be employed
outside the act of interpreting. The completion of
each task and incorporation of newly-honed skills
will generate a better work product.*

24. Observe Other Interpreters
25. Career Line & Skill Improvement
26. Analyze Your Work
27. How Do Deaf People Run Meetings
28. English Proficiency
29. Academic Language Models
30. But It's Not Polite to Curse
31. Vocabulary Resources
32. More Resources
33. Speech Outlines
34. Communication Vehicles
35. Deaf Interpreters
36. What's the Function?
37. Classifiers
38. More on Classifiers
39. English Transitions
40. ASL Transitions
41. Geography
42. Receptive Skills Development
43. Making Sense of Nonsense
44. Make a Conscious Decision to Evolve

24. Observe Other Interpreters

Watch another interpreter work in a setting in which you often interpret. Look for similarities and differences in how you handle the demands of that setting. Or enter a setting in which you want to become more familiar. If you often work in the courtroom or need to prepare yourself for the courtroom environment, get the necessary permission(s) required to observe the proceedings. Note how the interpreter approaches the bench and how the lawyers phrase their questions. Pay attention to the interpreter's work product. Request time with interpreters and ask why they do what they do. Request permission to watch a city council meeting, a computer class, a hearing and deaf team, and a (you-fill-in-the-blank).

25. Career Line & Skill Improvement

Today, use the space below to draw your interpreting career line as it relates to the advancement of your skills. (See the example on the following page.) Begin where your career first began. For example, start with the first time you met a deaf person or the day you graduated from an interpreting program. Include every event and sabbatical that impacted your skills. When did your skills spike, plateau, or decline?

Next, plot the future of your career. What might your future hold? Contemplate the possibilities and dare to dream.

Sample Career Lifeline & Interpreting Skills Improvement Track

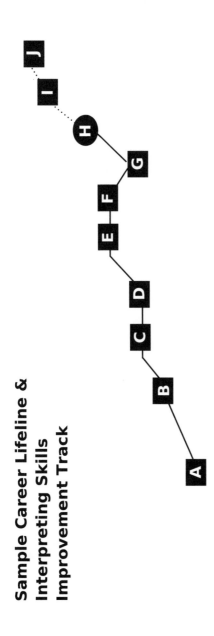

A) Training program graduation, started freelance interpreting. B) Took job as substitute teacher at school for the deaf. C) Plateau of skills. D) Took a job as a staff interpreter for agency that serves the Deaf and hard of hearing population. E) Plateau of skills. F) Left the field of deafness for a brief stint. G) Started freelancing again. H) Today. I) Join a mentorship program. J) Teach workshops to peers.

26. Analyze Your Work

Take a good, hard look at your work. Take a sample of your signed work, and analyze your interpretation. You can do this by videotaping yourself signing the news. Transcribe three minutes of your best work into ASL gloss. One week later, analyze the videotaped sample of your work by imagining being on the receiving end of your interpretation. First, look for errors with the sound still turned off. Are you signing in English word order? Does your interpretation make sense in the order it is signed? Do you notice any patterns of mistakes? For example, do you habitually omit information if you do not understand the message? Can you read your own fingerspelling? Now turn the sound on. Is the message equivalent to the source (the news)? Ask a peer or mentor to review your work in return for your review of his or her work.

27. How Do Deaf People Run Meetings?

If you have never interpreted for a board meeting in which the members use ASL as their official meeting language, go watch one in action. If the members use a voice interpreter for visitors/non-signing attendees, watch the work conducted in that setting. Pay close attention to how the board conducts business. Specifically look for how members: 1) open the meeting, 2) approve previous meeting minutes, 3) take turns communicating information, 4) move from old business to new business, 5) call for a vote, and 6) adjourn the meeting.

Look at logistical decisions regarding copy signing/mirror interpreting, seating arrangements, and the location of signers with regard to providing maximum visibility. By gathering this information, you will be better equipped to interpret the next board meeting you work.

28. English Proficiency

Proficiency in English is necessary for successful interpretations. Consider enrolling in an undergraduate or a basic adult English writing and comprehension course. Join a book club, or read books written by eloquent authors. Listen to books on tape. A strong English foundation will enable you to better articulate the abundant subtleties encountered when working among other languages and cultures.

29. Academic Language Models

Attend a residential school lesson taught by a fluent language model. Request permission to observe a teacher instructing a math lesson, a social studies lesson, or an English lesson. In addition to specialized vocabulary, watch for topic introductions. Learn how lists and diagrams are used. How is the in-class work assigned? How is homework assigned? What are the classroom turn-taking behaviors? Consider what you have learned and how the information can be incorporated into your own classroom-interpreting work.

30. But It's Not Polite To Curse

Practice voicing and signing curse words. If, as a child, you had your mouth washed out with soap when you used swear words, you might experience a sudsy taste every time a client curses when you are interpreting. Impolite words may make us stutter or alter our interpretation by omitting the curse words or signs altogether. So today, close your eyes and imagine an interpreting scenario in which both parties are cursing at each other. Remind yourself that this is not *your* message. If you chose to omit or water down the content, you deprive a person of free speech, and in some instances, you can even prohibit an opportunity for learning important social lessons.

The caveat is that some signs can appear to be curses when, in fact, they are not curses in English when properly interpreted. Assess the person's intent and body language, and include the setting in your assessment. If the curse sign is also mouthed as a curse in English, then it is probably safe to assume the person means that particular colorful word.

31. Vocabulary Resources

The National Association of the Deaf administers the Captioned Media Program (CMP). The CMP, among other things, has a free-loan media program with over 4,000 open-captioned videos, CD-ROMs, video streamers, and DVDs. CMP has sign-terminology videos such as, "Technical Signs: Physics" and "Twelve Steps and Twelve Traditions."

In addition, the CMP has instructional materials such as, "What is Biology," a 1996 open-captioned 25-minute video geared for grades 10-13+. Borrow this video before you begin work in a biology class so you can learn to identify the structure of DNA as a double helix before you have to interpret the information.

32. More Resources

Expand your knowledge by reading the "Bibliography & Suggested Materials" section of this book. Select one book, video, or CD-ROM to review. Consider reviewing one a month until you have exhausted the list. Purchase these materials, possibly sharing the cost with a peer, use an inter-library loan program, or the CMP.

33. Speech Outlines

Today, contact everyone in your assignment book who is giving a presentation and request a copy of his or her outline, speech, or lesson plan. Include presentations for students in any stage of their academic career. Read the material at least one day before its presentation. You are more likely to remember important information if you are able to sleep on it. When reading the presentation, look for and practice names, dates, spellings of key words, and the overall tone of the presentation. Identify the main point or points of the presentation. Look for areas where you are unclear about the point, and ask for clarification from the presenter before the job starts.

This preparation will improve the accuracy of your interpretation and help ensure smooth transitions between topics throughout the presentation. Can you sign/voice everything you expect might come up? If not, begin researching the topics by re-reading the text, using the Internet, and/or finding a peer to help you with vocabulary.

34. Communication Vehicles

Can you readily describe the similarities of and the differences between ASL, PSE, gestures, mime, oral communication/Oralism, Cued Speech, tactile communication, SEE I and II, the Rochester Method, LOVE, and CASE? If the previous sentence looks like acronym salad to you, your next task is to seek materials that delineate those similarities and differences. You will then be better equipped to facilitate communication by recognizing subtle, if not notable, clientele language use differences.

35. Deaf Interpreters

Take a look at your clientele. If you are a hearing interpreter, how many deaf clients would benefit from the use of a deaf interpreter? Be honest with yourself, but do not underestimate your skills. Do not consider only those consumers with limited language proficiency. Imagine how it would be to work with a deaf interpreter during a storytelling job. (It's great.) If you suspect a deaf interpreter will improve the interpreting product, contact your referral agency, your supervisor, or the hiring bean counter and tell them so. If you must negotiate, tell them you will split your fee until they see the often-tremendous benefits to all parties involved.

36. What's The Function?

Before your next assignment, identify what each participant might intend to accomplish by his or her interactions. A doctor helps patients by first asking questions (function of the questions: to identify the problem), then discussing solutions (function of the discussion: to generate ideas to alleviate that problem). A patient explains symptoms (function of the explanations: to offer information the doctor can use to diagnose) in order to alleviate those symptoms (the ultimate purpose behind the message). While interpreting, remember why everybody has been called together. Consider what information will be explicit and what will be implicit or implied. A doctor says, "What brings you here today?" Your signed interpretation might look like this: WRONG WHAT? ME-HELP-YOU, HOW?

If you consider the reasons people are saying or signing their message, you will frame your interpretation in such a way so as to convey the purpose behind the message. To put it another way, you are not only interpreting what is said and signed but also the functions of the interactions.

37. Classifiers

Recognizing and producing correct classifiers takes practice. In ASL, classifiers are handshapes (with particular palm orientations) representing nouns, noun groups, a noun's action and location, and a noun's physical characteristics (Baker-Shenk & Cokley, 1991). Saunders (2003) suggests that interpreters can improve their use of classifiers by recording a televised sporting event. Practice using classifiers by replaying the video using the slow-motion setting and using classifiers for each action shown. When practicing classifiers, Saunders adds, remember to include the appropriate facial expressions. Practice will improve your ability to both recognize and produce classifiers used in ASL.

38. More on Classifiers

Showing size, shape, depth, and texture, classifiers display physical characteristics of nouns and groups of nouns. Use classifiers to describe everything in your house. Lazorisak (2003) adds you can incorporate different viewpoints. Sign as if you are a bird looking down from above. Then, sign as if you are under the floorboards. This practice will make memory retrieval easier the next time you interpret the contents of a house.

39. English Transitions

Changes in and transitions between topics are challenging for many interpreters. Foster your skills with English transitions by listening to a television or radio personality. How do they articulate topic changes? On a piece of paper, list the ones you hear.

40. ASL Transitions

Plan a visit with your language mentor to work on ASL transitions. Discuss transitions between topics and the many ways ASL shows such changes. Armed with this information, you will have the vocabulary necessary to convey subject changes in your interpretation. Watch a fluent signer. How does he or she show topic changes? On a piece of paper, list the ones you see and practice them when you get home.

41. Geography

Geographical features of the areas where you interpret are likely to come up in the course of your work. Practice describing your immediate area and signing directions so that your memory-retrieval time is faster when it comes time to interpret that information. Show the rivers and mountains. Practice placing famous landmarks in relation to those rivers and mountains. Incorporate the highways and streets. Remember to place items according to *your* north, south, east, and west. Practice, by yourself or with a mentor, giving directions to and from different locations. Finally, ask a language mentor to ride in your car and give you driving directions in sign language, thus allowing you to see how language is used in a real situation.

42. Receptive Skills Development

How does an interpreter improve his or her receptive skills, the ability to understand a signer's message? First, use the space below to identify areas of greatest concern to you. Do you have more problems with fingerspelling, pronouns, or numbering in ASL? Do you have problems with specialized vocabulary or with transitions between topics? Once you've established a list, prioritize your challenges and look for resources to improve your skills. Locate a fingerspelling skill-building videotape. Find another videotape, and look only for pronouns or transitions between topics. Watch live signers, and look for the skill you want to improve the most.

43. Making Sense of Nonsense

Today, reflect on times you were unable to understand a message or part of a message. There will be times when your consumers do not make sense. Sometimes the hearing teacher fails to tie all of his or her instruction points together. Do not do it for him or her. There will be times, frequently in mental health settings, when deaf consumers do not make sense. You might be tempted to mistake language dysfluency for a deficit in your own comprehension. You might be tempted to make sense out of nonsense. We can spin some pretty creative stories with consumer's nonsensical signs. When you are not able to find topic cohesion or meaning, consider using third-person interpreting. Tell the mental health clinician, "He just signed DOOR, PHONE, BOWL, and another sign that I do not recognize."

It is the clinician's job to assess the significance of the message and to follow up as necessary, not yours. If it does not make sense, it does not make sense. Consider how you can transition into and use third-person (narrative) interpreting the next time the need arises.

44. Make a Conscious Decision to Evolve

Look for workshops. One characteristic of interpreting that keeps us in the field is our sustained interest in the diversity of the information we interpret. Each day brings a new challenge, and that means our knowledge base must be as diverse as the world in which we work. Get as much training as possible outside your assignments so that your work product will be more accurate. Look for interpreting workshops as well as workshops in other disciplines. Seek out conferences in arenas you find yourself working most often.

chapter three

Interpreting Newsspeak

"In order to stand a good chance of understanding what is being said, the interpreter must have some basic knowledge of the subject under discussion." (Seleskovitch, 2001) Becoming current is a strategic step on the road to message comprehension.

45. Where Was That Again?

Did you ever figure out where Bosnia or Kosovo was located? Is Iraq to the east or to the west of Iran? You don't have to tell anyone your answers (or lack of answers). Find a map and memorize one continent's countries. I recommend starting with countries that have been in the news most recently. Do the same for each continent until you can easily recognize many of the countries within the continents and their respective locations. If you do not own or wish to purchase a map, maps can be found in your local library and on the Internet.

46. Signs for the World's Countries

Today, get a world map. Sign the names of as many countries as you can. Then, visit a peer or language mentor and learn the ones that you did not know.

47. Multiculturalism

Have you heard the phrase "forty acres and a mule"? I hadn't until a Deaf, African-American man used it in a speech. His point was to show the African-American audience that Caucasian interpreters are not always aware of significant historical and cultural aspects of their life experiences. And he was right. I did not comprehend what he was saying, even after he signed it three times. Thanks to the important lesson he taught me, I recommend you secure training in multicultural affairs.

Mindness, Holcomb, Langholtz, and Moyers (1999) explain we must study American culture because, in order to interpret, we must be well-versed in the assumptions and conventions of the populations in which we work. They go on to say we must be able to identify the largely unnoticed cultural influences and biases in ourselves so we can prevent our baggage from seeping into the interpretation. Consider looking for information on the following unique populations: African Americans, Chinese Americans, European Americans, Japanese Americans, Korean Americans,

Mexican Americans, Native Americans, Puerto Rican Americans, and Vietnamese Americans. And there are so many more. When armed with background information about your own population as well as populations different from your own, the accuracy of your interpretation will undoubtedly improve. If the population you work for is heterogeneous, locate resources that promote an understanding of populations the same as, and different from, your own.

48. Computer Technology

Technology changes daily. If they have not already, computers are likely to influence your work at some point. Open a computer program, any program, and look over the options from Open to Exit. If you do not own a computer, go to your local library and use theirs. If you feel 100 percent computer- savvy, then go back to the computer again. Practice signing each step from booting up to shutting the computer down. You can learn technical signs by borrowing videotapes from video lending libraries and by finding a language mentor.

49. Current Events

Educate yourself regarding current, local, and world events. Read a newspaper today. When you pull up at the gas station to fill your tank and get a double-shot of caffeine, pick up a newspaper while you're at it. You can read it while you are waiting for your next assignment. This information will come in handy when the conversation drifts toward current events. If you understand the events being discussed, you can spend less processing time on semantics and more on the structure of the languages into and from which you are interpreting. In addition to picking up your local newspaper, subscribe to Deaf Community and interpreting periodicals, listen to talk radio stations, and look at news sources on the Internet.

50. Do Your Eyes Glaze Over When They Discuss the Economy?

What is the difference between a bear and a bull market? What in the world is a NASDAQ? Would somebody please explain the Dow Jones industrial average? What is the Index of Leading Economic Indicators, and if the Index goes up, is that a good thing? Today, if you do not know the answers to these questions, look them up.

51. Secretary of Who?

Become familiar with your state's governmental system. Today, get on the computer and look up your state's officials, starting with your governor. In the search box, type "(your state) government homepage." Today, look specifically for names and positions. An informed interpreter produces a more accurate interpretation.

52. Laws Regarding Deaf People & Education

Since much of our work is in the field of education, we benefit from basic knowledge about laws that affect the parameters in which we work. Are you familiar with the Education for All Handicapped Children Act (Public Law 94-142) or the Individuals with Disabilities Education Act (IDEA) (Public Law 101-476)? Have you read the 1997 amendments (Public Law 105-17)? Have you ever looked at the Americans with Disabilities Act of 1990 (Public Law 101-336) in its entirety? Do you have a working knowledge of the No Child Left Behind Act of 2001 (Public Law 107-110)?

People make reference to these laws, but do not always know how they apply to our work. Today, search the Internet for information about these laws.

chapter four
Semantics Skills and Thrills

*H.R. Haldeman said, "We are getting into
semantics again. If we use words, there is
a very grave danger they will be misinterpreted."
Tasks outlined in Chapter 4 highlight work
interpreters can do in the area of semantics.*

53. Signing Once or Twice?

No repeating signs today. Follow the linguistic features of signs so you do not create meaning or noun/verb pairs when you do not intend to do so. Pay attention to how many times you sign each concept. Sometimes we create meaning that does not exist in the source message. An easy mistake interpreters can make includes the use of YES, NO, and SHOULD. If a speaker simply and without emphasis says "yes," we might erroneously sign YES++++, emphasizing a point that was not emphasized by the speaker.

Other times, we inadvertently change the meaning by creating nouns when we mean to create verbs. For example, FLY could easily become AIRPLANE if you sign it more than once. CHAIR, a noun, and SIT, a verb, are signed differently. Clearly articulate the difference.

54. Interpreting Commonly Used Signs: COMMUNICATE/COMMUNICATION

Consider the ASL gloss for COMMUNICATE/ COMMUNICATION. What does a self-identified, culturally Deaf person really mean when they sign that concept? Consider the following common scenario: A hearing clinician with limited exposure to deafness is working with a Deaf person. The clinician says, "You want to have an intimate relationship, so why can't you write notes back and forth if the other person can't sign?" The Deaf person responds with, COMMUNICATION + IMPORTANT. PAPER + N.G. COMMUNICATION, in this instance, means so much more than the way it is used in the following interpretation, "Communication is important, and paper is not good."

Meet or call a peer, deaf or hearing, and discuss possible interpretations. Marla Broetz and Lori DeWindt (personal communication, September 2, 2004), both Deaf, suggest interpreters consider such issues as equality and English fluency. Your goal is to make what might appear implicit become explicit by finding a better, more complete interpretation.

55. Interpreting Commonly Used Signs: DEAF INSTITUTE

Consider the ASL gloss for DEAF INSTITUTE. What does a self-identified, culturally Deaf person really mean when he or she signs that concept? Consider the following scenario: You are interpreting for a group of three – two Deaf people (Rosella and John) and one hearing person (Lynn) who has limited exposure to deafness. The three are discussing and comparing high schools. Lynn asks, "So, John, where did you go to school?" John proudly responds with, "TEXAS + DEAF INSTITUTE."

What does that really mean? "I went to a deaf school in Texas" might not quite catch the full meaning. Instead, you might say, "I attended a residential school with students who are culturally Deaf and where my teachers and peers all used the same language."

Play with this one, and see what you come up with. Meet or call a peer, deaf or hearing, and discuss possible interpretations. Once again, your goal is a more complete interpretation.

56. Completing Your Sentences

Today, when voicing a signer's message, focus on completing each sentence. When voicing, have you ever started voicing one sentence (the first signed concept) and then ended that sentence with another (the second signed concept)? For example, a signer explains: "I was going to the refrigerator to get my diet yogurt. But, I got sidetracked and brought out the chocolate and marshmallow ice cream instead." If an interpreter voices, "I went to the refrigerator and brought out ice cream," the interpretation is missing a large portion of the message.

Another example of a mistake interpreters can make is to start voicing the above example with, "I went to the refrigerator... (pause)... But, I got sidetracked and brought out ice cream." Not only was information omitted, but the first sentence was not the complete sentence as signed. Be prepared to take more control over the flow of information. Pay attention to producing grammatically complete sentences if the source was grammatically complete. This is a good time to use your team interpreter. Ask your team to monitor your sentences and tell you about your use of English.

57. Good Ole Receptive Skills

To improve your recognition and use of ASL grammar, watch a video or videos with native signers. For this task, do not attempt to analyze patterns of use. Simply enjoy the stories and absorb language.

58. Pronoun Usage

Consider your use of pronouns, the words or signs used in place of nouns. For example, you might identify Leslie once, and then refer to Leslie as "her" or "she" thereafter. In your work today, be very clear about who is doing what to whom. When voicing for a signer, use words that clearly identify the person or people being discussed. For example, you will say, "Mrs. Henry made a pie for Mrs. Watson," as an alternative to, "She made a pie for her." When signing, clearly identify the noun and refer to it by pointing to it, gazing in its direction, or otherwise directing the conversation around it. From time to time, reiterate the noun to reconfirm its identity.

59. Sign Directionality

In ASL, signs can be used directionally by using our sign space to set up two people interacting. Example of directional verbs are: GIVE-TO, HELP, LOOK-AT, TELL, LEND/BORROW, SAY-NO/ YES-TO, etc. Just who is kissing whom? Today, make sure your directional verbs are going the right direction.

60. No Shortcuts –
Spell Proper Nouns, Names, & Cities

Today, fingerspell all proper names and proper nouns with the exception of regional signs typically used in your geographical area. Spell names of cities, titles of movies and books, brand names, television shows, and classes. It does save time to use signs; however, it is linguistically correct to spell them out. One temptation is starting a six-worded title by spelling the first three words and then using signs for the rest because it is quicker and easier. Today, avoid all shortcuts.

61. Borrowing Personas & Proper Affect

We often take on a person's character when interpreting something said or done. Do you accurately recount what was said or done while including his or her mannerisms? Do you portray how someone feels by adopting his or her mannerisms and facial expressions? And when role shifting, do you use your facial expressions to clearly show who is speaking?

Good role changing can decrease the need to name or identify the speaker, saving time that can be better used conveying the message. Today, work on borrowing the speaker's persona to more effectively communicate his or her message.

In addition to the overall persona, using accurate affect is an important task. Watch out for affect that is inconsistent with the signed or spoken meaning. When the angry boss is yelling, what is your face doing? Is your face flinching when you sign, "You are fired"? Affect mismatches can be obvious (like the example) or very subtle. Today, strive to interpret the affect as accurately as possible.

62. Political Correctness:
Language Deficits or MLS?

While still up for discussion, a person identified as a person with Minimal Language Skills (MLS), by some, is now being identified as a person with language deficits. You might say, "This person's language lacks certain linguistic components normally found in American Sign Language." If the other party wants more information, they can ask for your explanation. Today, consider the shift in perspective and its implications for your interpreting work.

63. Let's See How Many Letters
We Can Jam Into One Word

When fingerspelling today, include no extra letters or extra numbers in your work. For example, T-E-C-H-N-O-L-O-L-O-G-Y and D-R-A-G-L-O-N each have extra letters. In addition, avoid beginning a fingerspelled word and, after noticing you added a few extra letters, signing to the recipient, YOU KNOW. They may or may not know.

chapter five

It Takes a Village
to Raise an Interpreter

Language and interpreting mentors are
effective tools used by successful interpreters.
And while it is true that one person can paddle a boat,
two, three, and four paddlers will get there a lot quicker.

64. Securing Mentors

Do you have a mentor? If not, today consider getting one or even several mentors. Before choosing mentors, prepare by readying a list of your strengths and a list of skills you want to improve. You can have one mentor to work on vocabulary and another for topic transitions. A mentor can monitor your use of ASL glosses in your English interpretation. You can use a mentor to discuss particularly sensitive situations, knowing and ensuring that confidentiality shrouds the conversations.

Some interpreters living in rural areas will have a more difficult time locating a mentor. Knowing this, mentors can still be found and used. Look for mentors in your own community, surrounding areas, and at workshops. If proximity is an issue, tape or videotape your work and mail it to your mentor. Finally, because mentorship takes time, try to find a way to reciprocate the favor.

65. Are You the Chauffeur, the Schedule Reminder, or the Interpreter?

Some interpreters (as if our jobs weren't hard enough) are willing to take on more than one role with the deaf people with whom they work. Are you one of them? Are you routinely driving people to and from their appointments? Are you calling to remind people of their appointments? Are you consistently sure you know what's best for them and telling them so? Are you convinced you are the *only* interpreter who can work with *your* clients?

If so, consider the reasons you believe these things. How do you benefit, or what do you get from these beliefs and behaviors? Do you feel a sense of superiority or the satisfaction of helping those poor, poor hearing people and those poor, poor deaf people – people who cannot have any communication without you? This might be a difficult pill to swallow for some.

If you answered "Yes" to any one question, consider finding the fast track to mentorship. Might I challenge your thinking by saying that the hearing population and the deaf population have been coexisting for eons without interpreters? And, just like you were trained, another interpreter can be trained to work with consumers on your caseload. Choose someone you trust as a mentor to ensure both brutal honesty and the ability to handle your feelings without damaging your self-esteem. Investigate why you feel the way you do, and consider alternative options to the above-mentioned thoughts and behaviors.

If you are not engaged in these behaviors, but know someone who is, consider opening a dialogue with that person for the purpose of opening his or her eyes to a boundary they may not know they are crossing.

66. Unnecessary Fillers

Find a mentor to work with you on unnecessary verbal fillers. When voicing for a signer, are you often prone to using "uh," "um," and "you know" to fill awkward silences? If it is not present in the signer's presentation, it should not be present in your interpretation. If you notice yourself using the fillers, stop speaking. Repeat the sentence. And let silence reign. The silence will give your mind a chance to catch up and will give the listener time to digest the information just spoken.

67. Political Correctness: Gender, Sex, Race & More

In this day and age, more people focus on politically correct terminology. This trend holds true when voicing and signing. You will have to make choices for "Black" versus "African American," "Deaf/Hard of Hearing" versus "hearing impaired," and "handicapped/disabled" versus "someone who uses a wheelchair."

Signs evolve, too. Signs such as AFRICA (the shape of the continent) and GAY (fingerspelled) are more politically correct than their predecessors. Before working with a signer, explain that you want the interpretation to be voiced as he or she intends it to be voiced and that you need to start a dialogue regarding the signer's preferred sign choices and English interpretations.

Moreover, educate yourself about sexist language. In ASL, the gender of a person is not necessarily specified, so we can clarify the information by asking the gender or by using gender-neutral language. For example, we can say "chairperson" instead of "chairman." Today, discuss these and other politically correct concepts with a language mentor.

68. Sex & Drug Vocabulary

At times, lectures, treatment, and/or court cases we interpret may include information about sex and/or drugs. To interpret these often sensitive messages accurately, and to minimize the risk of appearing biased, learn the vocabulary before you enter the work setting, in lieu of learning them on the job.

Signs of Sexual Behavior (Woodward, 1979) and *Signs of Drug Use* (Woodward, 1980) are two books available for your reference. For a more current resource in CD-ROM format, locate the *American Sign Language Video Dictionary and Inflection Guide* (2000) produced at the National Technical Institute for the Deaf. View the sections titled "Socially Restricted" and "Substance Abuse."

69. Number Sign Systems

ASL has many number sign systems, and how you sign numbers is contigent upon the topic being discussed. Monetary numbers are signed differently than house address numbers. Baseball bases are signed differently than a number on a uniform. Locate *Numbering in American Sign Language: Number signs for everyone* (1998) published by DawnSignPress. The book describes number systems for how many, finances, measurements, time, frequency, ages, sports, scientific numbers, and more. If you do not have access to the book, find a number system mentor and improve your expression of numbers in your signed interpretation.

70. Raising the Interpreting Bar

Raise the bar today for interpreters in your area. Head a discussion group on cultural complexities related to interpreting. Start an interpreting book and video club. Discuss new theories about interpreting. Invent hypothetical ethical dilemmas and identify possible resolutions. Write a grant establishing a local mentoring scholarship program. Identify interpreters willing to be in the program, and outline their strengths. Set it up so each interpreter has an opportunity to be a mentor and an opportunity to be mentored.

Dubin et al. (2003) offer a recipe for successful mentorship programs for seasoned interpreters: First, assemble up to eight like-minded colleagues who share a need for mentorship. Second, schedule structured meetings in advance and assign one or two members to facilitate each discussion topic. Third, open mindedness and enthusiasm are two elements integral to the success of the group.

Dubin et al. state benefits to this type of mentorship include a safe, specialized forum for sharing, CEU opportunities, deeper professional relationships, and continuous improvement and growth.

chapter six

GOOOOO, TEAM!

Philip Caldwell said, "The important thing to recognize is that it takes a team, and the team ought to get credit for the wins and the losses. Successes have many fathers; failures have none."
A successful team of interpreters will use items outlined in Chapter 6 as a springboard into doing great teamwork.

71. Time for a Switch

When teaming, switching typically occurs every 15 to 30 minutes and the time varies according to the material being interpreted. Before beginning, agree to a set time and *stick to it*. Do not replace your team member too early or too late without good reason. If you replace too early, the interpreter being replaced may assume there is a reason, causing unnecessary tension. Before the job, discuss reasons for switching earlier or later than agreed.

A good reason to replace early is if you notice an increasing amount of errors in the interpretation or if she or he asks to be replaced early. A good reason to replace later than the agreed-upon time happens when the material being interpreted would flow better by letting the actively working interpreter finish the concept (waiting for a natural break such as the end of a slide or between speakers) before the switch.

72. Requesting Support

How do you typically request support from your team interpreter? Some interpreters tilt their heads or lean into their team interpreter to indicate their need for information. Some use direct eye contact both to tell their team they have missed information and to ready themselves to receive the missed information. Try to specifically identify the missing information, such as a date, a name, or a monetary amount. On occasion, in a desperate attempt to get support, you'll hear about a panicked interpreter throwing a microphone to their team.

I did that once. Fortunately for me, my team did not hit me over the head with the microphone. However, my action did bring the Deaf man's presentation to a halt. He had to wait until we could get it together and get caught up before he could go on. Today, consider your preferences and be ready to tell your team how you are likely request support.

73. Receiving Support

Decide how you prefer to receive a feed, or support, from your team interpreter, in the event you need assistance while actively interpreting. (No, being fed in this circumstance does not involve grapes or doughnuts.) If you miss information, do you want the key words whispered in your ear? Do you want information signed in ASL? Do you want it signed in English word order? Do you want your team to produce the correct interpretation and then allow you to continue the interpretation? Do you want one word or a full, complete thought? Do you want a 2-foot by 2-foot blinking neon sign? Today, consider your preferences and be prepared to share the information with your team interpreter before your next teaming assignment.

74. Memory Quirks

Did you know that people have a tendency to remember the first and last items on a list and often forget what's in the middle? Today, keep that in mind and pay a little more attention to the middle items on a list. Knowing this quirk will help you more effectively support your team interpreter because you now know which items are more likely to be forgotten.

75. Whispering

Today, ask your team interpreter to monitor your vocal output when you sign. Sometimes when we transliterate and are articulating English words on our lips to facilitate speech-reading, we are unaware of the smallest whisper escaping our throat.

76. Smooth Interpreter Exchanges

Switching interpreters is noticeable. Before the assignment and to minimize the disruption, discuss with your team interpreter the manner in which you will be switching. Will you walk behind your team and tap a shoulder? Will you stand on the side of the room and wait for them to notice you? Will you sign READY from your seat to indicate it is time to switch interpreters? If so, communicate with your team to avoid any misunderstanding about switching activities.

And, in conclusion, I may suggest that you discuss exchanges beforehand and establish an understanding between team members. When your team indicates they are ready to take over, you should trust that they are ready to pick up exactly where you leave off. Complete your thought and step aside to let them work.

77. Distracting Noises

Today, ask your team interpreter to monitor sounds made by your movement (feet shuffling), signs (hand-to-body impact), or clothing while working. If you learn you are making noises, make changes to minimize or eliminate the sounds.

78. Requesting & Offering Feedback

Today, consider the importance of team feedback. You might begin a conversation with your team interpreter by saying: "Today, I would like to work on my use of space. If my use of space is inadequate, please leave me a note or find a way to tell me to broaden my use of sign space."

Be wary of giving unsolicited feedback to your team. If your team does not request your feedback, refrain from giving your well-meaning golden nuggets. You never know how your team will feel about your feedback, nor do you know how they will perceive your intentions.

With that said, as part of a team, you must always give feedback if the interpreted message is inaccurate. All team members are responsible for the accuracy of the message. You are required to give feedback that corrects incorrect interpretations.

79. Final Note on Teaming

Today, focus on the elements that make you a good team player. Lewis and Muroski (2003) offer numerous tips for successful team interpreting. The following information is a condensed version of their conclusions: A good teammate arrives on time, wears a watch, and stays the entire length of the job. A good teammate prepares for assignments and calls if he or she needs to cancel. A good teammate participates while in the "off" role, monitors the message, and knows how to request and give feeds. Finally, a good teammate will share his or her preferences and is open to suggestion.

Today, consider the above-mentioned tips and plan to incorporate them into your work.

chapter seven

Taking Care of You

*Interpreting is a demanding job, and to succeed,
we must be at the top of our game. To be successful,
thriving interpreters incorporate self-care items
outlined in Chapter 7.*

80. Reducing Sign Force

While signing, reduce the applied contact force of hand-to-hand or hand-to-body contact. When you are signing, reduce the amount of sudden, jarring pressure inflicted by your signs. Examples of signs to observe are STOP, SCHOOL, MY/MINE, TABLE, PAPER, etc. If you can hear a "thump," "smack," or any other noise, then you need to reduce the pressure in that sign. Contact force, sending shock waves through your body, can result in injury if done repeatedly. If your goal is emphasis, try using non-manual markers.

81. On A Bad Day

Had a bad interpreting day and wonder why? First, do not jump off the closest curb. Due to the nature of the job, we all have "off" and "I'm-so-hot-I'm-on-fire" days. Reflect back on what worked and on what did not work. What needed changing? What will you do next time? Remember that everyone involved in the situation is responsible for communication – not only the interpreter. So spend time and energy on reflection, and then go eat some ice cream.

82. Definitive Fees

Independent contractors, state your fee with poise and confidence! Have you seen the cognitive processing models of sign language interpreting? If you have not, your next task is to find one or two and study the complexities of our work (Cokley, 1992, p. 124; Colonomos, 1992). Our jobs are intrinsically complex and entails numerous demands. If you do your job right, you use lots of gray matter. As independent contractors (or self-employed businesspeople), interpreters often have to supply their own health insurance, 401 (k) plans and retirement benefits. You attend workshops, read books, and watch videos to maintain and enhance your skills. In addition, many interpreters today seek higher education. So in actuality, our fees are not so high. Flip your hair, and tell yourself, "Because I am worth it!"

83. The Cost of Business

Calculate the cost of doing business today. Calculate how much you are earning today. Subtract mileage and taxes. Time on the road and the time it takes to fill out the timesheets often go unpaid. If you are so inclined, consider ways to generate money and improve your cost efficiency. Develop a self-marketing plan to get more, or higher paying, work. Minimize your costs while maximizing your paycheck.

Multi-tasking is one way to maximize your time. While sitting in traffic, you can return phone calls (if legal in your state). While sitting in the waiting room, check your e-mails and secure pending jobs on your latest electronic gizmo. Read the speech you were just handed for tomorrow night's presentation while waiting for today's clients to assemble.

You may also want to consider reserving specific days of the week for driving to and working in nearby towns. Minimize your travel between towns as much as possible. Hit the library to find a list of tax-deductible items, and then make sure to run them by your tax guru at the end of the year.

84. Opportunities for Improvement

What skills are you trying to improve upon? Today, sit down and outline your list of objectives. Then make a plan to address each one. Upon which skill or skills do you want to focus attention, and how do you intend to go about it? How will you measure improvement? Who will help you? Make a contract with yourself, and include realistic deadlines. Finally, reward yourself for your hard work when you succeed.

85. Rest Your Hands

Today, rest your arms and hands as you work. You can drop your hands to your side if you're standing or into your lap if you're sitting, instead of adopting the "prayer" pose. You want oxygen-rich blood flowing to your hands and fingers. These brief breaks may reduce the incidence of repetitive stress injuries, so give your hands a rest when you can.

86. Pain Evaluation

Today, evaluate your pain after interpreting and consider keeping track of your pain for one week. Do you feel discomfort, numbness, burning, cold, shooting pain, weak, tender, hot, itchy, or stinging? Range your pain from 0 (*no pain*) to 10 (*severe or unbearable pain*). Is your sleep disrupted due to pain? If yes, you may consider seeing a physician about Cumulative Trauma Disorder (CTD) or Repetitive Stress Injury (RSI). CTD/RSIs are responses to the excessive demands we place on our bodies without giving them adequate time to recover. If diagnosed with a CTD/RSI, possible treatments include splints, anti-inflammatory drugs, and physical therapies such as cold packs, electrical stimulation, and relaxation exercises.

As with most ailments, an early diagnosis will give you a better chance of a quick and full recovery. At the very extreme end, if left unattended and if problems worsen, you may be forced into another vocation. Take care of yourself, even if it means you cut your hours or change your workload for a period of time.

87. Voicing Nerves

How do you feel about voicing? If you cringed when you thought about the question, you probably have anxiety. Anxiety can manifest itself in different ways. We rapidly shift in our chairs, and our heads bounce from one shoulder to the other. We scratch nonexistent itches. Our legs kick out and pull in only to go back out again. Some interpreters lean forward eight inches for a better view. Our body has crafty ways to display our nervous innards.

So how do you alleviate anxiety before the voicing job, during the job, and after the job? Some interpreters, not unlike presenters, take three minutes of silence to get centered before the job. Some find better living through chemistry (anti-anxiety medications), and still other interpreters prefer to stretch in a quiet place. Reduce your caffeine intake. Breathe from your abdomen instead of your upper chest before and during the assignment. Finally, tell your team interpreter your needs and ask him or her to watch for indications that you may be shutting down.

88. Certification

Some states have certification systems while others do not. Do you have certification? If not, why not? If yes, have you passed at the highest level obtainable? If not, why not? Today, make two lists. The first list outlines the benefits of taking and passing a state or national interpreter certification test. Maybe you will get a raise in pay or a self-esteem "promotion." Maybe your peers will see you as an equal, and consumers will have more confidence in your abilities. The second list outlines reasons not to take or retake a certification exam. Exams can be cost prohibitive and the fear of failure is real. Include personal, professional, and more global reasons to take or retake an exam on both lists. Today, your only charge is to closely examine all aspects of taking or retaking an examination.

89. Insurance

Today, assess your insurance needs and your current coverage. What types of insurance do you carry? Do you have liability, health, dental, vision, or worker's compensation? If your referral agency or employer offers no insurance, consider securing insurance coverage elsewhere. Your preparedness might save your bank.

90. Interpreter Bags

Many interpreters carry supplies in bags or backpacks. These supplies can come in very handy (pun intended), including the following: planner, water, lotion, hand sanitizer, tissues, glasses/ contacts and contact solution, flashlight, anti-inflammatory medication, parking tags, ID badges, tomorrow night's speech (in the event you have a free moment to skim it), mints and/or cough drops, snacks, business cards, and anything else you might need for your specific brand of interpreting.

In addition, consider keeping the following items in your already fast-food littered, jam-packed car: a phone book for times when you get lost, laminated maps of the towns and campuses you frequent, and a set of non-wrinkle clothing for last minute assignments.

91. Slouching

Many interpreters slouch. Slouching puts your body out of balance and causes your limbs to be stretched or bent awkwardly. If you slouch, you can go to the gym to improve your posture. To improve your posture, you first need to find out why you slouch. There are several reasons why someone can have poor posture. Go to a gym and consult with a fitness expert. If poor posture is due to lower back or abdominal muscle weakness, work on those muscles. If it is because your upper chest is overdeveloped, you may need to work on your middle back, rear delts, traps and lats.

When interpreting, your posture should be relaxed with no slouching or leaning. Sit against the back of the chair. Your legs should be uncrossed and you should have both hips placed squarely on the chair. Your feet should be flat on the floor or supported by a footrest. And remember to take frequent breaks.

92. Seeing Behind You

Do you ever wish you could see the discussion points projected onto the screen behind you? Consider purchasing a mirror developed specifically for interpreters. These mirrors allow you to see slides projected behind you, television and videotaped materials, and math equations being written on a board. The equipment has two mirrors. The first one captures the image behind you; the second one reverses the image so it reads right to left. When you can see the information to which the speaker is referring, your job will be easier and the accuracy of your interpretation will definitely improve.

93. Invoices & Cards

If you are an independent contractor or want to become one, what does your invoice look like? Do you have a business card to offer a potential or current customer? You may be more likely to get repeat business by handing your card to someone as you leave an assignment. Cards and invoices can be elaborate or simple. You can go to a professional and have them made, or you can make them yourself on your home computer. Collect cards and invoices from your peers, and use the samples to help you generate your own unique design. In addition, look for materials developed by interpreters that outline invoice and marketing guidelines and suggestions. See Fisher (1998) in the "Bibliography & Suggested Materials" section.

94. Diagnostic Assessments

Investigate the possibility of purchasing a diagnostic assessment of your work. Performed by trained professionals, an assessment provides an objective evaluation. Ask around your interpreting community for names of assessors. If there are none in your community, broaden your search to surrounding areas and states. An assessment will detail your strengths and provide you with a list of opportunities for improvement. They can start around $100 and normally require a videotaped sample of your work. Information gleaned from an assessment can make you a better interpreter.

95. Water

Drink water today. Dehydration compromises your ability to pay attention to detail. Take a small bottle of water to each job today. If the bottle is with you, you are more likely to drink it. Add lemon slices or juice to your water if you are more likely to drink it with flavoring. In addition to assisting your brain, water acts as a cushion and keeps your tendons mobile.

96. Limit the Length of Time Interpreting

Depending on the job, an interpreter should not interpret for more than one-and-a-half to two hours alone. In addition, interpreters put themselves at risk for injury if they work 21+ hours each week. Maybe you have already noticed that when your arms and hands hurt, your sign clarity is compromised. Have you ever switched to signing with your non-dominant hand because your dominant hand hurt from signing too long? If you answered "Yes," then big red flags are going up just for you. You are expending mental energy to keep the pain at bay – energy that could be better used to produce a more accurate interpretation.

If this situation happens, tell all parties that you need a break, stop interpreting, and leave the room. If the participants wish to continue without you, they can write, type on a computer, or use any other method of communication they wish until you return. If you suspect a job might go long, you should request a team interpreter before the job begins, or inform your clients you might need a break. Tell them when you are likely to need the breather so they will not be surprised when you request your break.

Discuss your concerns with your employer and arrange your jobs so you have frequent breaks.

97. Physical Safety

Today, consider the following points for your personal safety. When interpreting at night, walk your team interpreter to their car and let them drive you to yours. When working in mental health, consider getting an unlisted phone number. Give people general locations of your home, not an address. Take a self-defense course. Wear clothes that enable you to move quickly. Wear shoes that protect your toes and the safety goggles they give you. Buy a personal alarm. Place a first-aid kit in your car. Use instant hand sanitizers. Purchase equipment that will allow you to contact others in the event you have car trouble. Finally, and maybe most importantly, trust your instincts.

98. Money Matters

Taking care of yourself includes taking care of your money, too. Many interpreters work as independent contractors and also for referral agencies. Some jobs reimburse for mileage, while others do not. We eat at fast food places and toss the receipts into our glove box. We purchase invoices, stamps, business cards, computers, and cellular phones. We go to workshops and pay for certifications. Today, schedule an appointment with a local tax accountant or Certified Public Accountant. Ask about the laws in your state and for an explanation of the differences between *independent* and *employee* status and what that means for tax filing purposes.

Devise a system to keep track of every stamp you use to mail an invoice. If you drive one mile to a job, do you have a way to keep track of mileage? Driving one mile three times a week for one year is worth more than $50 at the time of this writing. Fifty dollars may not seem like much until you add in the cost of food, stamps, planners, gas, car maintenance, phones and phone bills, workshops, books, invoices, business cards, and office equipment.

99. Emotion-Laden Work

We can be called upon to work in extremely personal situations. It is not uncommon for us to see people at the worst times in their lives and to share their pain through our work. What do you do after an especially emotional job? Do you have a safe place to process your grief, anger, frustration, anxiety or other distressing reactions? Do you pretend nothing happened, or do you hold it in waiting for the emotions to slowly drain away?

If you have strong reactions, you are not crazy, weak, or alone. I recommend one or a combination of several of the following self-care options. Try exercise or yoga. Spend time in nature. Seek mentorship or establish a self-help group for interpreters – a safe place to process feelings while helping others in your same situation. Journal your emotional reactions (omit all client-identifying information). Contact your spiritual advisor. Engage in recreational activities such as art and music to express your feelings in a positive, creative way. And, if you believe it to be necessary, seek counseling.

chapter eight

Getting Out of the Way

Chapter 8 offers unique insight into the many ways interpreters interject themselves into the interpretation and offers avenues to minimize such intrusions.

100. Controlling Your Reactions

Today, assess to what extent *you* enter into the interpretation and work on your reactions. Your opinions about the content being interpreted can generally predict how you may inadvertently show your reactions during an interpretation. At your job today, focus on yourself within the interpretation. Do you react in any way to the people or subject matter? Do you disagree with one person's comments or agree with another's, revealing your alliance with subtle frowns or nods? Are you rolling on the floor, belly-laughing, before interpreting something humorous?

Make a mental list of jobs you cannot work due to personal reasons or value differences. For example, if you have strong feelings about a church denomination, a political party, or the people at the job site, you might involuntarily show your reaction while in the act of interpreting, thus influencing the outcome of the event.

Next, make two more mental lists. Make a list of jobs in which you may, but aren't likely to, have problems, and a list of jobs you can sail through without blinking. Although we are more likely to accept the latter two of those three job categories and therefore less likely to have personal biases influence our work, we still need to consciously practice controlling our verbal and nonverbal reactions.

101. Clothing Choices

Our job allows us variety in clothing choices. Monday, we wear a suit in court. Tuesday, we wear overalls for factory training. But, whatever you do, don't wear overalls in court. Consider these tips when dressing for success:

Wear pigment-contrasting shirts so your hands are readily visible. Minimize accessories so interpreted messages are understood (not missed because your earrings or wild necktie were distracting). No short shorts in the classroom and, for safety reasons, women should avoid dresses and high heels when doing mental health work. Save glitter eye shadow for interpreting music concerts. If you feel the need to express yourself, paint your toenails fire engine red instead of your fingernails.

Due to the limited number of encounters the general public has with interpreters, our clothing choices reflect on our entire profession, as well as those who use our services.

102. Open Up Your Sign Space

Focus on your use of sign space and how it may affect communication. If you usually limit everything you sign to one square foot, you may consider enlarging that space. If your signs are too small, it may be difficult to understand the interpretation (Taylor, 1993). Small sign space also has emotional connotations of fear and/or embarrassment. Deaf consumers may think the interpreter is embarrassed to sign in public (especially older deaf consumers). Your hands need to be seen and easily readable. By opening your sign space, you can, in fact, improve the chances for clear communication.

To open your sign space, try sitting or standing with your shoulders squared and your head back. Relax your posture. Instead of using only your hands and wrists, include your arms and shoulders, too.

103. Visual Noise

When interpreting, be aware of extra body movements. Do you often find yourself shifting your weight, touching your face, or pulling your bangs out of your eyes? Are you chewing gum or repeatedly checking your watch? Does your head bounce like a bobble head? Visual noise can be distracting. Today, pay attention to extraneous movements. When emphasizing a point, use your eyes and eyebrows instead of leaning forward. If you have a team interpreter, ask him or her to identify and count extraneous movements. Today, be a minimalist.

104. One- or Two-Handed Signing?

Do you regularly use one hand for a sign when you should be using two? For two-handed signs where both hands are symmetrical, one individual hand carries more information than it does for two-handed signs where the hands are asymmetrical or differently shaped (Battison, 2003). Two examples are FLOOR (symmetrical) and BANANA (asymmetrical). By using two hands, especially for asymmetrical signs, you minimize the chances of miscommunication and make your signs easier to read. Today, use one hand for all one-handed signs and two hands for all two-handed signs.

105. They Just Didn't Get It

Have you ever left a job thinking one party was extremely dense or just didn't get it? Consider another source for their confusion. You. If you saw or heard something that both parties were not made aware of, something may have been lacking in the interpretation. When working, identify and interpret seemingly implicit information that, if clarified, would make both parties better understand each other.

Sometimes, in spite of a nearly perfect interpretation, the consumers still don't get it. After analyzing your work for strengths and weaknesses, move on. Do not obsess about something over which you have no control.

106. Why Sign What Can Readily Be Seen?

When interpreting for yoga, exercise, algebra or some other visible concept, allow the addressee the opportunity to watch the actions of the instructor. Stop signing and refer them to the instructor. You waste time and energy when you explain something they can readily see. Plus, when looking at the instructor, a one-on-one direct connection can be made between two people without the interpreter.

107. Relaxing Your Shoulders

Today, interpret with your shoulders down and in a relaxed position. If your shoulders are hunched up, it can give the impression that you are either very excited or very scared. And while some jobs can be both exciting and scary, shoulders that are too tight can restrict the size and ease with which you use your sign space. If you find difficulty relaxing your shoulders, try stretching before stressful and/or stage assignments. Stretching will increase the blood flow into your muscles and increase your range of motion.

Ask a professional for specific exercises for your neck and shoulders and for stretching your torso and legs. And though it may seem self-indulgent to some, regularly scheduled massages can help keep your muscles loose and can help to prevent injury.

108. No Yawning

Stay alert. Refrain from yawning while interpreting (J.E. Clark, personal communication, July 29, 2003; Hoza, 2003). Yawns, normally lasting about six seconds, are distracting and they convey disinterest. Even if it is the sixteenth new employee orientation that month, try not to appear bored. Conveying boredom indicates you have an opinion and we strive to keep our opinions out of our work. If you feel the urge to yawn, take a deep breath, drink your water, or shift your posture. At the next break, stretch your body to increase your blood pressure and your heart rate. In addition, flex your muscles and your joints. Feel free to yawn good and strong, flexing your jaw and face muscles during that break. Finally, if you know you are in for a long day, get plenty of rest the night before.

109. Equal Opportunity Dislike

Some interpreting situations become heated debates. Providing equal access means you have allowed two people to not like each other if they so choose. When faced with the option of softening a message that does not produce warm, fuzzy feelings or saying/signing it like you hear/see it, opt for saying/signing it exactly how you perceive it. If you struggle with interpreting for parties that disagree and/or dislike each other, try to remember this situation has nothing to do with you. You may not be privy to prior interactions between the two people, and your decision to soften the message can have damaging ramifications.

You are the messenger. And if I am correct, in these situations the messenger is not normally shot. So, if the situation calls for it, deliver the message with a bang.

CHAPTER 9

Special Considerations & Everything Else

"While the public at large believes that an interpreter's job consists of learning and using a lot of words in different languages, for the interpreter the problem of language is only one component part of a much larger whole."
(Seleskovitch, 2001)

110. Paper & Props

Today, consider how the use of props may help to ensure clear communication. Do not be afraid to get a pen and paper to draw pictures to get a point across. This strategy can be particularly helpful when working with people who have limited fluency in ASL and/or English. Because your job is to transmit information between two parties, the needs of your clients should dictate the form of that transmission.

For example, when securing a consumer's follow-up appointment with a doctor, use the strategically placed desk calendar by pointing to the exact date of the proposed appointment. When interpreting for a job training, consider showing the expected task instead of signing the task. Finally, be prepared for the additional time it may take to draw pictures, point to information, and demonstrate job tasks.

111. Breaking Eye Contact to Take Notes

Deaf people may take notes during meetings. Unless otherwise instructed, when they look down, wait until they look up before interpreting the next chunk of information. We strive to make our interpretation clear and understandable. If you hold the information now, your subsequent interpretation will be easier because you will have fewer gaps to fill in. In other words, you will not have to work as hard to provide a comprehensible interpretation because you waited to give the person all the information and laid a foundation upon which you can build as new information comes in. Plus, waiting, when you can, is just plain courteous.

112. Eyestrain

Sometimes deaf people look away from us to reduce the eye fatigue that can be experienced after a long day of interpreter watching. While they rest their eye muscles, take advantage of the extra processing time. The additional processing time is likely to improve your work product. If this occurs, do not take it personally and continue interpreting unless otherwise instructed.

113. Forgettable Fact

Hoffman (2000) reports that on average we forget 80 percent of what we learn on any given day. So when you forget a consumer's name and/or where you met them and he or she asks, "Don't you remember you interpreted for my son's graduation?" you have a ready-made response. You can say, with all honesty, you do not remember the event and then share Hoffman's interesting statistic.

114. Hot Potatoes

Has a deaf consumer ever given you information that you believe should have been told to his/her clinician? Once before an appointment at a mental health facility, a client told me he would lie to the clinicians and tell them he did not believe the television communicates with him when, in fact, he believed it still did. Because I made myself available before the job, I left myself open to being tossed a hot potato — information for which I did not want to be responsible.

While what you do with a hot potato will depend upon the information you are given, you can be proactive and do everything you can to prevent being placed in an awkward position. Today, imagine telling a hearing clinician that you cannot stay in a room with a consumer if no interpreting is necessary. You can say, "I will leave with you." Or say, "They may tell me something they should be telling you, and because I may not know what is clinically relevant, I will stand outside the door until you go back in." You can explain there are liability issues to consider and that you prefer to wait outside or that your agency stipulates you leave any situation that has the potential to become a liability issue.

115. Diverse Language Use

Due to the diverse nature of the deaf community, you may find yourself working for two or more deaf clients who have two or more language/mode preferences. For example, one may prefer all information mouthed and signed in English word order while the other prefers ASL. Instead of signing one, then the other, and working twice as hard to meet both clients' needs (often causing a breakdown in the interpretation process), when feasible, ask the clients to choose one mode or language or somewhere in between.

A warning: Whether ASL, English word order, or somewhere in between, signed communication choices are often accompanied by strong philosophical and personal biases. The selection of one person's preference over another may shift a delicate balance of power in a room.

116. Interjecting A Consumer's Comments

How do you choose to interrupt a fast-paced conversation amongst hearing meeting members to incorporate a deaf participant's comments? This is a time when your suave cultural mediation skills come in handy. You can say: "Excuse me. Louis would like to go back to a point Mike brought up a minute ago." Or you might say, "Mrs. Hammer has a comment." Then wait until the group acknowledges Mrs. Hammer.

Another solution is to simply interject the comment and wait until the group acknowledges the comment. In many instances, nobody else waits for recognition before they comment. They throw comments out and see what happens.

Today, think of three to five more ways to interject a comment. Once you have different phrases in your toolbox, they will be easier to retrieve when you need them.

Caution: Be sparing with your index finger directed at a deaf consumer to indicate "Wait a moment." Even if you are simply waiting for the hearing culture's appropriate moment, it could be construed as offensive and/or oppressive.

Consider nodding to the deaf participant indicating you understood the point and will interject the comment as directed.

117. Third-Person Interpreting

You will, on occasion, encounter hearing people who have no frame of reference for deaf people, interpreters, and the work interpreters do.

To clarify my point, I'll give an example. To tell Steve (who never met a deaf person before) what Martha (who was born deaf into a deaf family) is signing, begin with third-person interpreting. For example, to Steve you might interpret, "Martha says she is interested in learning more about the project you are currently developing because she is working on a similar project and would like to compare notes." Had you started in first person by saying, "I am interested," Steve may think you are the interested party.

If you start in first person, you put yourself in a position that requires an added statement explaining it's Martha, not you, who has opened the dialogue. Starting in third person will help you avoid being in that position.

118. I'm Going Somewhere to Work With Someone & Will Be Home Sometime Soon

Besides government spies, what other profession requires complete silence regarding the whereabouts of its workforce? When your significant other asks where you are going today, your answer *can* depend on how restrained he or she can be when someone calls and asks for your whereabouts. It also depends on the state in which you live. For example, in Missouri, interpreters are allowed to tell their significant others the location of the job and not much more.

When you tell your significant other you are going downtown to the hospital, how much information can he or she actually glean? Today, consider the limitations placed upon our profession in your state and reflect upon the implications of telling those closest to you where you are going. Include consideration of your personal safety.

119. Backseat Interpreting

Resist the temptation to backseat interpret. If you are not part of the interpreting team for an event you attend, unless the working interpreter has requested your assistance, sit quietly and remind yourself that you are not on this job. If you believe you have caught a word/concept that the working interpreter missed or misunderstood, resist the sometimes powerful urge to join the conversation. Do not blurt it out and do not sign it.

There are several good reasons to keep quiet. If you feed a sign from your chair to the signing interpreter, you disrupt the interpreter's train of thought, and if a presenter notices the visual disruption, he or she might wonder what you are doing, and you will have successfully disrupted his or her train of thought, as well. If you yell the missed information from your chair, you run the risk of distracting the presenter, the interpreter, and the entire audience. You never hear about lawyers yelling out better courtroom strategies to lawyers trying cases. If you choose to join the conversation, people will remember you – not because you were the brilliant interpreter in the room with the correct interpretation but because you were the only one in the room who could not keep a lid on it.

120. Power

Interpreters have an incredible amount of power and with that power comes the equivalent amount of responsibility. We have access to incalculable quantities of commercial and private sector information. We are privy to an individual's most personal stories. And, with a simple head turn and an eye gaze, we can control the flow of information in a crowded room.

Can you see how our presence puts people, both deaf and hearing, at a disadvantage? A company executive may fear we will share the company's trade secrets. A deaf person may refrain from criticizing our work for fear of retribution at a later date.

To the people with whom we work, we must strive to convey we are grounded in doing our job both ethically and competently and are neither judgmental nor biased.

Today, when you go to work, assess your ability to influence the situation and look for places where you could, or someone might believe you could, misuse your power or manipulate the situation. Then, look for places where you can convey to them that their trust is well placed in you.

121. Who Are You, and What Do You Do?

Introducing yourself and explaining your position is a task interpreters encounter daily. Hoza (2003) suggests we prepare a thirty-second explanation of our role and function. What might you say?

To the receptionist: "Hello. My name is Marla, and I have been hired by the hospital to interpret for Dr. Farquhar and her client Mr. Sanders."

To the deaf presenter with an audience of six hundred, you might get right to the point by saying: "The American Philanthropic Association hired me to interpret your presentation to hearing audience members. I've reflected on your notes and understand your three main points are give, give, and give. Would you say that is an accurate description of your address?"

Today, look in your book and identify three jobs where you will practice and refine your role and function speech.

122. You Did Such A Wonderful Job!

The general public can be curious about sign language and will often ask you where you learned *while* you are working. After that immediate flash of, "Dang! I wish they didn't do that," you can choose one of several responses:

One, you can interpret the question to the deaf person, indicating the question was directed at you, the interpreter. This option allows the deaf person to either use the opportunity as a teaching moment by telling them you are a "communication tool... talk only to me..." or to allow you the opportunity to answer.

Two, you can answer and then quickly get back to your job, telling the deaf person what just happened.

Or, three, you can choose to ignore the question altogether. If you are leaning toward the third choice, you may want to think again. You are not invisible and you *are* in the room. You are one of three, not zero of two.

123. Those Same Old Questions

How do you respond when asked if you are the deaf person's sister, brother, or daughter? What do you say when asked why the deaf person is running late for their appointment? How do you answer when asked if deaf people are allowed drive, or if you can read Braille like deaf people? Am I pushing any buttons yet? Do you ever feel like getting cheeky and informing them their question lacks the common sense component?

As Witter-Merithew (1996) explains, we sometimes forget how far we have come. These sincere questions come from a person's need to learn more than they currently know. Because over the years, we hear the same questions and because many questions are paternalistic in nature, we might feel tempted to stick up our noses and impolitely answer their question or to ignore their question altogether.

Another approach would be to craft a response that is both polite and educational. To the woman who approached me after a job and emphatically suggested I wear white gloves when interpreting because they would look "neat," I said, "Oh, I hadn't thought of wearing gloves, but I believe they are sometimes worn in theatrical settings." Admittedly, before I responded, I had to discard the first two answers that came to me: "What?!" and *"That's* a new one!"

By responding politely to seemingly daft questions, we open a channel for dialogue. Your task is to list commonly asked questions and match them to answers that are both respectful and informative.

bibliography
& suggested materials

Baker-Shenk, C. & Cokley, D. (1991). *American Sign Language: A teacher's resource text on grammar and culture*. Washington, DC: Clerc Books, Gallaudet University Press.

Battison, R. (2003). *Lexical Borrowing in American Sign Language*. Burtonsville, MD: Linstok Press.

Calder, A. (2002). *Language and Learning Services: Study Skills: Organization: Mind Mapping: How to do a Mind Map*. Retrieved August 14, 2004, from the Learning Advisers in the Academic Support Division of James Cook University, Institute for Learning Technologies Web site: http://www.jcu.edu.au/studying/services/studyskills/mindmap/howto.html

Caldwell, P. (n.d.). *StudyWorld: Quotes by Author: C*. Retrieved August 15, 2004, from Studyorld/Oakwood Mgt. Web site: http://www.studyworld.com/newsite/Quotes/QuoteByAuthor.asp?i=c

Cokley, D. (1992). The Effects of Lag Time on Interpreter Errors. In D. Cokley (Ed.), *Sign Language Interpreters and Interpreting* (SLS Monograph, pp. 39-70). Burtonsville, MD: Linstok Press. (Original work published 1986)

Cokley, D. (1992). Interpretation: A sociolinguistic model. *Sign Language Dissertation Series.* Burtonsville, MD: Linstok Press.

Colonomos, B.M. (1992). *Processes in Interpreting and Transliterating: Making them work for you.* Riverdale, MD: The Bicultural Center.

Drucker, P.F. (n.d.). *BrainyQuote: Quotes by Author: Peter F. Drucker Quotes.* Retrieved August 15, 2004, from BrainyQuote, Xplore, Inc. Web site: http://www.brainyquote.com/quotes/authors/p/peter_f_drucker.html

Dubin, R., Finkbone, B., Moeller, J., Shaw, D., Sills, R., & Smith, M. (2003, July-August). Working Together Through Peer Information Exchange: Mutual Mentoring for Seasoned Interpreters. In *Our Nation and Profession: Working Together, 2003 RID National Conference Handout Book* (pp. 234-236). Symposium conducted at the meeting of the 18th National Conference of the Registry of Interpreters for the Deaf, in Chicago, IL.

Fingerspelling Practice Tapes: Fingerspelled loan signs [Videotape]. (1991). Burtonsville, MD: Sign Media.

Fingerspelling Practice Tapes: Geographic locations [Videotape]. (1991). Burtonsville, MD: Sign Media.

Fingerspelling Practice Tapes: Miscellaneous items [Videotape]. (1991). Burtonsville, MD: Sign Media.

Fingerspelling Practice Tapes: Proper names [Videotape]. (1991). Burtonsville, MD: Sign Media.

Fischer, T.J. (1998). *Establishing a Freelance Interpretation Business: Professional guidance for sign language interpreters (2nd ed.).* Hillsboro, OR: Butte Publications.

Haldeman, H.R. (n.d.) *BrainyQuote: Quotes by Author: H. R. Haldeman Quotes.* Retrieved August 15, 2004, from BrainyQuote, Xplore, Inc. Web site: http://www.brainyquote.com/quotes/authors/h/h_r_haldeman.html

Hoffman, D. (2000). *Who Knew?* New York, NY: MJF Books.

Hoza, J. (2003). *The Interpreter's Guide to Life: 365 tips for interpreters*. Burtonsville, MD: Sign Media.

Lazorisak, C. (2003, July-August). Self-Assessment: Cultivating your CDI professional skills. In *Our Nation and Profession: Working Together*. Symposium conducted at the meeting of the 18th National Conference of the Registry of Interpreters for the Deaf, in Chicago, IL.

Lewis, C.J. & Muroski, K.S. (2003, July-August). Team Interpreting: Making Each Other Look Good. In *Our Nation and Profession: Working Together, 2003 RID National Conference Handout Book* (pp. 183-188). Symposium conducted at the meeting of the 18th National Conference of the Registry of Interpreters for the Deaf, in Chicago, IL.

Lucus, C. Bayley, R. & Valli, C. (2003). *What's Your Sign for Pizza? An introduction to variation in American Sign Language*. Washington, DC: Gallaudet University Press.

Merithew, A.W. (1996, May 18). *The Socio-Political Context of Interpreting as Mediation* [Videotape]. Telecast at Sinclair Community College, Dayton, OH.

Metzger, M. (1999). *Sign Language Interpreting: Deconstructing the myth of neutrality.* Washington, DC: Gallaudet University Press.

Mindness, A., Holcomb, T.K., Langholtz, D. & Moyers, P.P. (1999). *Reading Between the Signs: Intercultural communication for sign language interpreters.* Yarmouth, ME: Intercultural Press.

National Technical Institute for the Deaf, Rochester Institute of Technology (Producer) & Poor, G.S. (Director). (2000). *American Sign Language Video Dictionary* [CD-ROM]. Rochester, NY.

Neumann Solow, S. (2004, January). *I Know What I'm Doing Wrong…What Am I Doing Right?* 22nd Annual Interpreter Symposium conducted at the California State University at Northridge.

Neumann Solow, S. (2000). *Sign Language Interpreting: A basic resource book (Rev. ed.).* Burtonsville, MD: Linstok Press.

Numbering in American Sign Language: Number signs for everyone. (1998). San Diego, CA: DawnSignPress.

Patrie, C.J. (Creator), Dannis, J. (Producer), & Lee, Y. (Director). (1997). *Fingerspelled Names and Introductions: A template building approach* [Videotape]. San Diego, CA: DawnPictures Video.

Patrie, C.J. (Creator), Dannis, J. (Producer), & Lee, Y. (Director). (2002). *Interpreting in Insurance Settings* [Videotape & Book]. San Diego, CA: DawnPictures Video & DawnSignPress.

Patrie, C.J. (Creator), Dannis, J. (Producer), & Lee, Y. (Director). (2002). *Interpreting in Legal Settings* [Videotape and book]. San Diego, CA: DawnPictures Video & DawnSignPress.

Patrie, C.J. (Creator), Dannis, J. (Producer), & Lee, Y. (Director). (2002). *Interpreting in Medical Settings* [Videotape and book]. San Diego, CA: DawnPictures Video & DawnSignPress.

Saunders, J.R. (2003, September). *Classifiers for Interpreters.* Seminar conducted at William Woods University in Fulton, MO.

Schirmer, B.R. (2001). *Psychological, Social, and Educational Dimensions of Deafness.* Boston, MA: Allyn & Bacon.

Seal, B.C. (2004). *Best Practices in Educational Interpreting (2nd ed.)*. Boston, MA: Allyn & Bacon.

Seleskovitch, D. (2001). *Interpreting for International Conferences: Problems of language and communication* (S. Dailey & E.N. McMillan, Trans.). Arlington, VA: Pen and Booth. (Original work published 1968).

Sign Media (Producer) & Cokley, D. (Director). (1992). *Interpreting the Miranda Warnings* [Videotape]. Burtonsville, MD.

Stewart, D.A, Schein, J.D. & Cartwright, B.E. (1998). *Sign Language Interpreting: Exploring its art and science*. Boston, MA: Allyn & Bacon.

Stratiy, A.P. & Taylor, M. (1998). *Pursuit of ASL: Interesting facts using classifiers* [Videotape]. Edmonton, Alberta, Canada: Interpreting Consolidated.

Taylor, M.M. (1993). *Interpretation Skills: English to American Sign Language*. Edmonton, Alberta, Canada: Interpreting Consolidated.

Taylor, M.M. (2002). *Interpretation Skills: American Sign Language to English*. Edmonton, Alberta, Canada: Interpreting Consolidated.

US Department of Education. (n.d.) Captioned Media Program. Retrieved on September 4, 2004, from http://www.cfv.org/

Winston, B. & Monikowski, C. (2000). Discourse Mapping: Developing Textual Coherence Skills in Interpreters. In C.B. Roy (Ed.), *Innovative Practices for Teaching Sign Language Interpreters* (pp. 15-66). Washington, DC: Gallaudet University Press.

Woodward, J. (1980). *Signs of Drug Use: An introduction to drug and alcohol vocabulary in American Sign Language.* Silver Spring, MD: T.J. Publishers.

Woodward, J. (1979). *Signs of Sexual Behavior: An introduction to some sex-related vocabulary in American Sign Language.* Silver Spring, MD: T.J. Publishers.

Valuable Internet Resources

ADARA, Professionals Networking for Excellence in Service Delivery with Individuals Who Are Deaf or Hard of Hearing: **www.adara.org**

Alexander Graham Bell Association for the Deaf: **www.agbell.org**

Association of Late Deafened Adults: **www.alda.org**

The Captioned Media Program: **www.cfv.org**

Clear View Innovations: **www.interpreter-mirror.com**

Conference of Interpreter Trainers: **www.cit-asl.org**

Deaf Resource Library: **www.deaflibrary.org**

Dogs for the Deaf: **www.dogsforthedeaf.org**

Laurent Clerc National Deaf Education Center: **clerccenter.gallaudet.edu/InfoToGo/ index.html**

National Association of the Deaf: **www.nad.org**

National Captioning Institute: **www.ncicap.org**

The National Dissemination Center for Children with Disabilities: **www.nichcy.org**

National Theatre of the Deaf: **www.ntd.org**

Rainbow Alliance of the Deaf: **www.rad.org**

Registry of Interpreters for the Deaf:
  www.rid.org

Self-Help for Hard of Hearing People:
  www.hearingloss.org